METAVERSE

and Other Virtual Reality Tech

Co-published by agreement between Shi Tu Hui and World Book, Inc.

Shi Tu Hui
Room 1807, Block 1,
#3 West Dawang Road
Chaoyang District, Beijing 100025
P.R. China

World Book, Inc.
180 North LaSalle Street
Suite 900
Chicago, Illinois 60601
USA

Copyright © 2024. All rights reserved. This volume may not be reproduced in whole or in part in any form without prior written permission from the publishers.

WORLD BOOK and the GLOBE DEVICE are registered trademarks or trademarks of World Book, Inc.

Library of Congress Cataloging-in-Publication Data for this volume has been applied for.

Cool Tech (set, hardcover)
ISBN: 978-0-7166-5479-7

Metaverse and Other Virtual Tech
ISBN: 978-0-7166-5483-4 (hardcover)
ISBN: 978-0-7166-5495-7 (softcover)
ISBN: 978-0-7166-5489-6 (e-book)

Written by Tom Jackson

STAFF

VP, Editorial: Tom Evans
Manager, New Product: Nicholas Kilzer
Curriculum Designer: Caroline Davidson
Proofreader: Nathalie Strassheim
Coordinator, Design Development & Production: Brenda Tropinski
Digital Asset Specialist: Rosalia Bledsoe

Developed with World Book by
White-Thomson Publishing LTD
www.wtpub.co.uk

ACKNOWLEDGMENTS

Cover	© CKA/Shutterstock	28-29	NASA/JPL-Caltech/MSSS; © Raymond Cassel, Shutterstock; © Boston Dynamics; © DOE Photo/Alamy Images; © Sueddeutsche Zeitung Photo/Alamy Images
5-9	© Shutterstock		
10-11	© Alexey Boldin, Shutterstock; © REDPIXEL.PL/Shutterstock; © Indiapicture/Alamy Images; © Raymond Asia Photography/Alamy Images		
12-19	© Shutterstock	30-33	© Shutterstock
20-21	© Time to Draw/Shutterstock; © PopTika/Shutterstock; © Soonios Pro/Adobe Stock; © elenabsl/Shutterstock	34-35	© Gregg Vignal, Alamy Images; © Gorodenkoff/Shutterstock
		36-37	© Facebook; © StockCanarias/Shutterstock; © Cultura Creative RF/Alamy Images
22-23	Pete Souza, White House Photo; © Peter Sobolev, Shutterstock	38-39	© Holodia; © Motion Metrics; © Anton Gvozdikov, Shutterstock
24-25	© Richard Milnes, Alamy Images; © Elnur/Shutterstock; © Piero Cruciatti, Alamy Images; © Leonel Calara, Shutterstock; © ZUMA Press/Alamy Images	40-41	© Shutterstock
		42-43	© David Gabis, Alamy Images; © Ground Picture/Shutterstock; © John D. Ivanko, Alamy Images; © WESTOCK PRODUCTIONS/Shutterstock
26-27	J.M. Eddins, Jr., US Air Force; © Restuccia Giancarlo, Shutterstock; © PaO_STUDIO/Shutterstock; © Haiyin Wang, Alamy Images	44-45	© Shutterstock

CONTENTS

Acknowledgments 2

Glossary 4

Introduction 5

1. In the Metaverse 6
2. Cryptocurrency 14
3. Telepresence 22
4. Metaverse Architecture 30
5. Everyday Life in the Metaverse 34
6. Super Senses 40

Resources 46

Index 48

There is a glossary of terms on the first page. Terms defined in the glossary are in boldface type **that looks like this** on their first appearance in the book.

GLOSSARY

app short for software application. A software application is a computer program that enables a human user to perform some task or activity.

artificial intelligence (AI) the ability of a computer system to process information in a manner similar to human thought or to exhibit humanlike behavior.

autonomous able to operate with little or no human control or intervention.

avatar an image created and manipulated on a computer screen to represent one's role in an online game or other cyberspace interaction.

blockchain a database of transactions that is shared across a digital network of users. Unlike a traditional database, a blockchain does not rely on any single entity to verify and store transaction data.

cryptocurrency a form of digital currency that relies on cryptography to remain secure. Cryptography is the translation of data into a code that only authorized users can translate back into readable language. Cryptography prevents the theft and counterfeiting of cryptocurrency.

greenhouse gas a gas that warms the atmosphere by trapping heat of solar radiation reflected from Earth's surface, much like the glass in a greenhouse.

hacker a person involved in the manipulation of a computer program, device, or system in a way unintended by its creator or owner.

haptic technology that can create an experience of touch for a user through forces, vibrations, or motions.

real estate land and all the things permanently attached to it, such as trees, buildings, and minerals beneath the surface. A house is real estate.

renewable energy from natural resources that can be used over and over. It includes energy from the sun, from wind, from moving water, from heat beneath the ground, and from plants.

ultrasound sound that is too high-pitched for human beings to hear.

virtual reality (VR) an artificial, three-dimensional (3D) computer environment. A VR experience is typically viewed through a headset. It replaces what a person normally sees and hears with computer-generated images and sounds.

INTRODUCTION

Computers are amazing tools, so amazing that one day, perhaps in your lifetime, they will create an entirely new world. This new world might feel as real as the one you are in now. However, it is located not in space but inside the memories and processors of vastly powerful computers. A world like this is science fiction today, but computer scientists are working to create it. They already have a name for it: the metaverse. This name comes from the words *meta*, meaning "beyond," and universe. The metaverse will only be limited by computing power—and not the laws of physics that control the real world. For example, gravity might work differently in the metaverse; we could change our appearance and size in an instant; and we could travel just by thinking about where we want to go. The sky is not the limit, because the metaverse never runs out of space. This new world would go on forever and contain anything we can imagine. How might such a world exist, and what would it be like to live in a computer? Let's find out some more about the metaverse.

1 IN THE METAVERSE

A NEW WORLD

The endless possibilities of the metaverse are exciting and perhaps a little frightening. And they are certainly mind-boggling! Everything that exists in the real world can be recreated in the metaverse. We can have a home, go to school, work at a job, and visit friends. If we want to watch a concert by our favorite singer or watch a sports team play, we can be there in the metaverse. Your entire community could be recreated in the metaverse, with your house, your street, and you neighborhood, but the Eiffel Tower and Grand Canyon could be down the road as well! But rather than an alternative reality that copies this one, the metaverse will allow people to live in completely new ways. We could break free from the limitations of our bodies. We could travel across space to Mars or Pluto, or even create a brand-new planet to explore.

LIVING IN CYBERSPACE

The metaverse sounds like science fiction. There is a good reason for that! The idea originally came from a 1992 novel titled *Snow Crash* by Neal Stephenson. In this story, the metaverse is a place constructed inside computers where people seek refuge from an unpleasant real world. That made a good story, but a real metaverse does not have to be a place just to escape troubles. The metaverse technology being developed today aims to make the real world a better place—cleaner, more efficient, and a lot more fun.

Future city. The metaverse depicted in the novel *Snow Crash* is a city built along a single wide highway that circles an imaginary planet. The "snow crash" in the title refers to a failure of the metaverse software that makes everything go white and fuzzy, like a blizzard. A futuristic city named Neom is under construction in Saudi Arabia. Neom is planned to be 110 miles (170 kilometers) long but only 660 feet (200 m) wide!

Avatar. A user of the metaverse is represented as an **avatar.** This is a computer-generated body that is controlled by the user in the real world. The term *avatar* comes from a Hindu term that refers to the form that a god takes when visiting Earth. In the same way, an avatar in the metaverse can take any form. However, an avatar must follow a set of rules. For example, the *Snow Crash* metaverse has a limit on how big an avatar can be, and no one is able to travel faster than they can in the real world.

Rules of the metaverse. There are other features needed for a metaverse. These ensure that it is more than a game or form of entertainment. The metaverse will be an alternate version of the real world. For example, the metaverse has many users acting independently. This is different from most video games, where a virtual reality is usually constructed around a single user. Time in the metaverse only goes forward, and users cannot travel back in time. Events take place in real time. In other words, separate events are happening all over the metaverse right now, and a user can only be in one place. You can still run late in the metaverse! The metaverse is also persistent. That means if a user leaves the metaverse for a while, they cannot pause or reset. The metaverse just keeps on going with or without them. A final rule is that the actions of the users have costs and benefits—not everything is free. Users in the metaverse must work for money to buy what they need, just like in the real world.

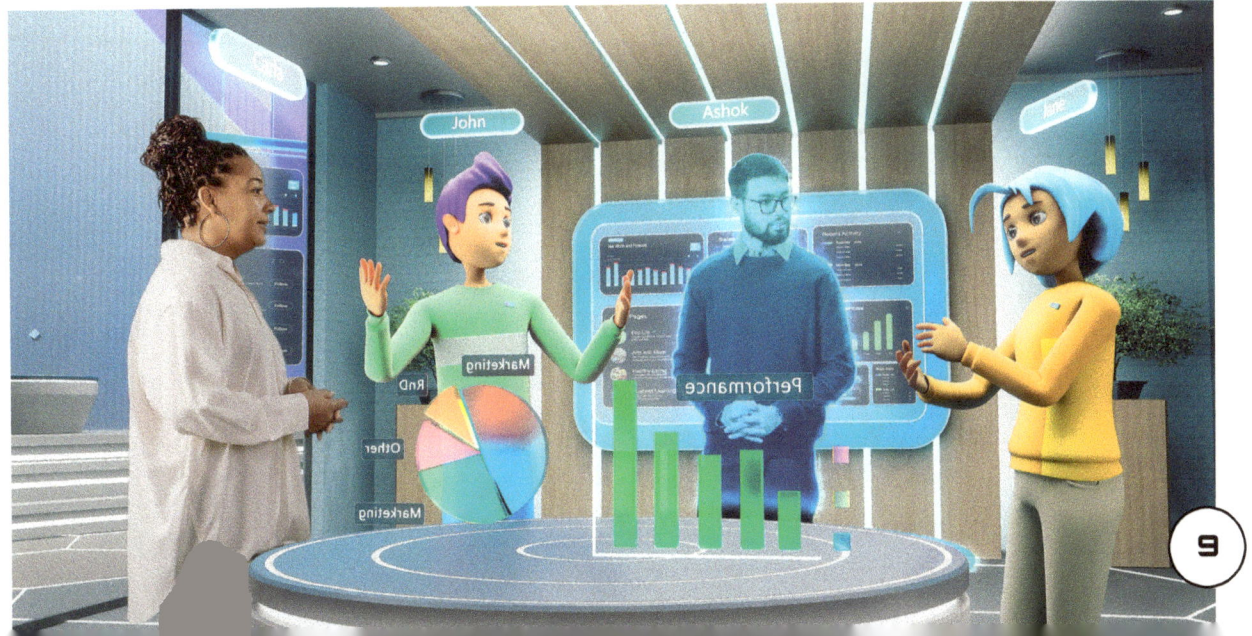

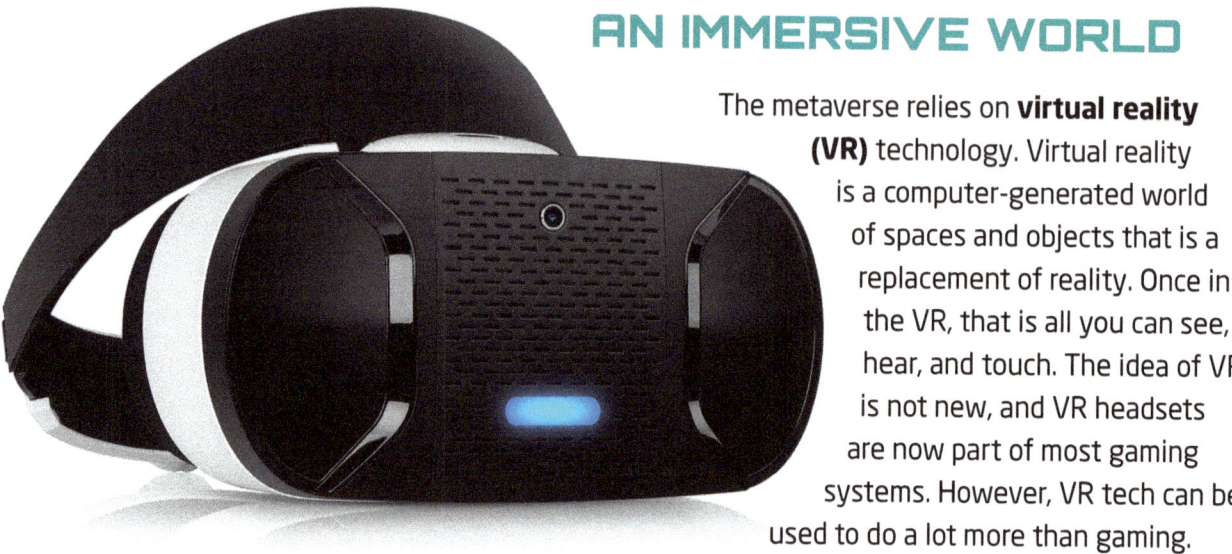

AN IMMERSIVE WORLD

The metaverse relies on **virtual reality (VR)** technology. Virtual reality is a computer-generated world of spaces and objects that is a replacement of reality. Once in the VR, that is all you can see, hear, and touch. The idea of VR is not new, and VR headsets are now part of most gaming systems. However, VR tech can be used to do a lot more than gaming.

Headset. The VR headset includes a video display, headphones, and a microphone. Each eye sees its own screen. The displays are offset so each eye picks up a slightly different view. The brain uses this difference to construct a 3D (three-dimensional) view of the scene. The headset tracks the motion of the user's head and adjusts the display accordingly, so that a user can look around the virtual surroundings. The latest headsets also track the smaller movements of the eye. Eye trackers pick up where the eye is focusing. Only the graphics in that part of the display need to be detailed. The rest can be blurred out because the eye cannot see it. This system reduces the computing power needed to create a metaverse.

Haptics. In the real world, objects have weight and texture. We feel these qualities using sensors in our skin that are squeezed and stretched as we touch objects. **Haptics** is the VR tech that recreates this sense of touch by pushing and pulling on the skin even though there are no physical objects there. This is called feedback. The most common haptic device is a glove, but the system works as a full bodysuit. Just like the headset, motion sensors called accelerometers are used to track the motion of the hand or body in space. If an avatar meets a VR object, the haptic tech creates touch feedback on the real body. It does this in different ways to make the feeling more realistic. For example, the skin can be fooled into thinking it's touching an object by little puffs of air or pulses of **ultrasound.** The suit also has mechanical actuators, small moving parts that can vibrate the skin or give it a tap.

Uncanny Valley. It will probably be impossible to recreate a VR experience that seems completely real using a headset, headphones, and haptic feedback alone. There will always be something wrong, and that creates the "Uncanny Valley" phenomenon. Technology is getting ever better at creating computer graphics or physical robots that look like living things. However, when these unreal copies get close to looking real, they fall into the Uncanny Valley, where suddenly they look strange, frightening, and even disgusting to us. Experts aren't sure why this happens. It might be that we will all be happier in a metaverse where the avatars are cartoonish or obviously nonhuman in some way.

ONLINE IDENTITY

For the metaverse to be a convincing world, it must obey some of the same rules as the real world. However, can we forget about the other rules that we live by? Can you steal and commit crimes in the metaverse? And if you did, would you get in trouble in the real world?

Authenticated users. The metaverse relies on the avatars of the humans that use it being authenticated. That means the system can match each avatar to a human in the real world. Just like humans in the real world, each avatar is unique, and only one can exist at a time. How much information about an avatar is visible to other users in the metaverse? In the real world, we are allowed to keep our names and other personal details secret. We get to choose who we tell that information. The same will probably be true in the metaverse. However, not every character in the metaverse has to be an avatar of a real human. Do you think it will be important to be able to tell human metaverse users apart from computer-generated features? In the real world, we can always be sure that the people we meet are real people!

NPC's and AI's. In gaming, the nonhuman features are called NPC's or nonplayer characters. The metaverse is not a game, but characters that function like NPC's could be included. The metaverse will provide some services automatically. A taxi or train does not need a human avatar to drive. When a user buys something from a store, they do not need a human avatar to pack the bag and hand it to them like in the real world. Instead, these characters in the metaverse would be NPC's. They are only there to make things seem more real and easier for human users. However, what if nonhuman avatars were smarter and more independent than this? These characters would be **artificial intelligence (AI)** creations that did their own thing. Perhaps human users could have AI servants or friends in the metaverse? Life in the metaverse sounds complicated, maybe even more so than in the real world!

Consequences. In the real world, society is governed by morals. This is a system that divides the actions of people into good or bad. However, our actions are not limited to the real world. We can do good and bad things online, too. Therefore, the same moral system will exist in the metaverse. It is usually simple enough to tell right from wrong. If someone does something bad in the real world, then society will punish them. The nature of the punishment depends a lot on the consequences of the action. Someone who drops litter is doing a bad thing, but the consequences are small. The problem can be fixed by picking up the litter. So the punishment for littering is small. Other crimes have more serious consequences that can never be fixed, so the punishment for that crime is severe.

Unreal crimes. Are the consequences of these actions the same in the metaverse? Is it even possible to litter there, and can an avatar be harmed? If an avatar can be harmed by another user so that it no longer works, its owner in the real world is nevertheless unharmed. Could the avatar just reload where it left off, or would the user need to create a brand-new avatar? The consequences of bad actions in the metaverse are much less than in the real world, and the punishments would probably be less severe, too. However, everything a user does in the metaverse is recorded as it happens, so punishments for their wrongdoing could be delivered automatically. In this setup, would it even be possible to break the rules and do bad things?

2 CRYPTOCURRENCY

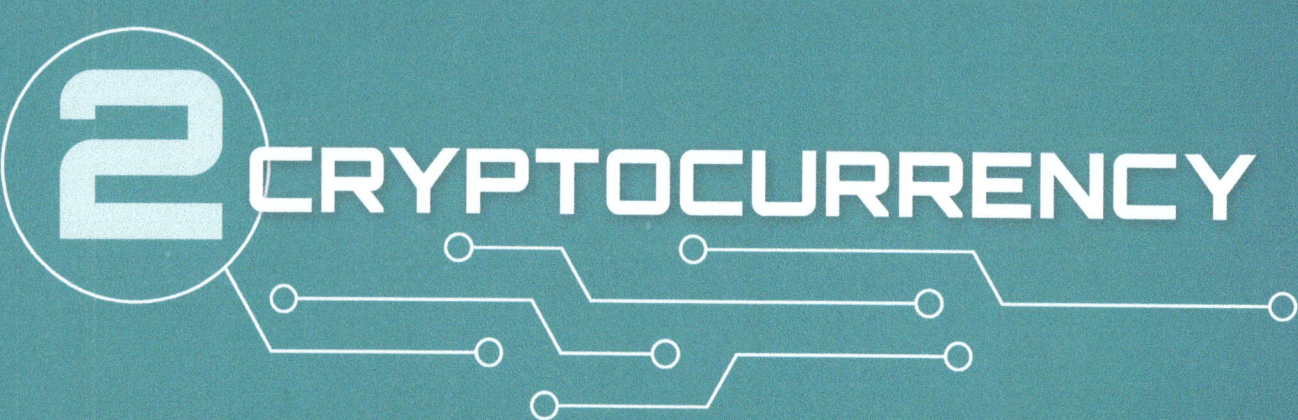

PROGRAMMED PLAYLISTS AND PERFORMANCES

"Money makes the world go round" is an old saying. It means that, like it or not, money is necessary for society. Nothing really works without it, and that includes the metaverse. However, money in the metaverse does not have to be the same as the money used in the real world. Instead of bills and gold bars locked away in bank vaults, the metaverse will probably use a system called **cryptocurrency.** Cryptocurrency has no coins or bills. It is stored on a computer. When it is spent, the system just changes the records of who owns the money.

Currency is a money system, and *crypto* means "hidden." However, that name makes the idea of cryptocurrency quite confusing. Regular money systems are run by governments, while cryptocurrency is run by the people that use it. Regular money is worth something because the government makes sure of it. Cryptocurrency must have another way of ensuring it has a value, or people would stop using it. Cryptocurrencies do this by keeping a record of every time the money is spent. That ensures that people cannot cheat the system and spend money they don't have. Some of the information needed to maintain this record or ledger is part of the cryptocurrency that has to be kept hidden for the system to work. The person who owns the cryptocurrency is also a secret. But the system should work fine even if that information was public. A cryptocurrency ledger uses a system called a **blockchain.** The metaverse will use blockchains for more than handling money. A blockchain is a way to make sure every avatar is a human and that everyone in the metaverse is following the rules.

DIGITAL CASH

The oldest and most famous cryptocurrency is Bitcoin. This cryptocurrency originated in 2009 and remains the most popular and valuable cryptocurrency. The second most popular cryptocurrency is Ether, the currency of the Ethereum system. Both work in different ways. Which one will be best for the metaverse?

Cyber money. It is not possible to withdraw a Bitcoin or an Ether from the bank and carry it around in your wallet or purse. The currencies are just lines of code stored on a computer. In some ways, that makes them just the same as most of the money in the world. Only about 8 percent of the world's money exists as cash—coins or bills. The rest exists only in banking records stored on computers. In this way, a bank in the metaverse would be no different from a bank in the real world.

Miners. A single bitcoin is a long number code. This code is unique to each bitcoin and contains information such as where it is stored and when it was created. New bitcoins are made by "miners." Instead of digging in the ground for bitcoins, miners use their computers to solve complicated math calculations. The correct answer to this calculation is the code for a new bitcoin, which now belongs to the miner.

Limited supply. Every time a new bitcoin is mined, the calculation needed to make a new one gets slightly more difficult. The system is organized so that there can only be 21 million bitcoins. After that, the calculation needed to make the next one would take a computer forever to solve. Bitcoin is organized like this to make sure it stays valuable. Gold is valuable because it is rare, and there is only so much of it to buy and sell. That same fact makes bitcoin valuable. The Ethereum cryptocurrency does this in a slightly different way. It can never run out, but only 18 million Ether can be produced in any single year.

Environmental cost. Cryptocurrencies are very big business, and miners use powerful computers to access them. Experts estimate that about 0.75 percent of all the electrical power used in the world is now used for mining cryptocurrency. That is more than the energy used by all of Argentina or Australia. Some miners have their own power supplies, and some are using **renewable** energy. However, the current operation of cryptocurrencies produces a lot of pollution and **greenhouse gases.**

BLOCKCHAINS

Cryptocurrencies rely on a database called a blockchain. Blockchain records everything about the currency, including every time one is mined or spent. It contains a huge amount of information that is changing constantly and must never be wrong! That is where the miners come in. Their computers check and update the blockchain over and over again.

Distributed computing. If a blockchain were stored in one place, it would be vulnerable to attacks from **hackers.** If a hacker could change the records on the blockchain, the hacker could create money or steal it from other people. To prevent that, the blockchain is spread out over millions of computers. These are the computers of the miners and other people that use the cryptocurrency. The information stored on one computer is useless without all the other bits. Hackers would have to attack all the computers at once, which is impossible.

All in agreement. Blockchains were developed for cryptocurrencies, but they can be used to hold all kinds of information. The important thing is that everyone agrees that the information stored in the chain is correct. Today, this is done by cryptocurrency miners. Every record of a transaction is checked by the mining computers. The human miners cannot see that information. It exists only in the form of uncrackable codes. The computers use math to show that the information is correct. Every 10 minutes or so, the latest updates add up to a new packet of encoded data called a block. The database is a long and ever-growing chain of these blocks.

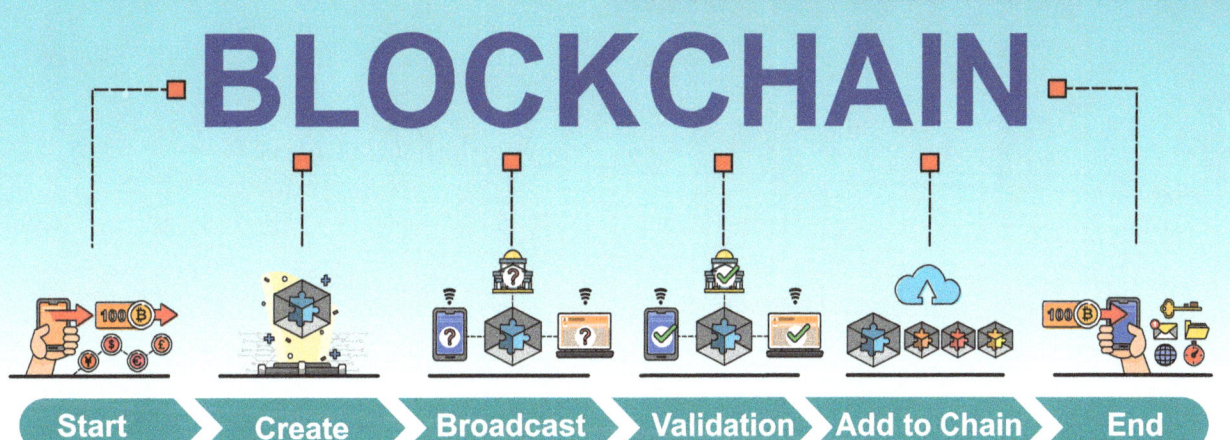

Staking a claim. The system of maintaining blockchain uses huge amounts of energy—which is bad for the environment. But there is another way to run a blockchain that does not need so much computing power. This system is called proof of stake (PoS). The Ethereum currency uses PoS, while Bitcoin uses proof of work (PoW). In PoW, a miner must do all the work needed to validate the blocks and earn a coin. Several miners may race to do it as fast as possible. Only one wins, so the energy of the others was wasted for nothing. PoS uses validators, not miners. Validators hand over some coins as their "stake." This earns them the right to validate blocks and earn more coins. Fewer validators are needed, and so less computing power and energy is used. They also check each other, and if one cheats they lose their stake.

IDENTITY AND PROPERTY

The metaverse, with all its important rules, will only work correctly if there is a database recording the actions of each user. With millions of users, this is going to be a huge set of data. A blockchain is the best way to keep track of it all. Many experts say that a metaverse can only work if a blockchain is there to make sure everything is fair and no one cheats.

Authentication. Miners and validators make cryptocurrencies work by maintaining the blockchain. In return, the blockchain allows the miners and validators to earn cryptocurrency. A similar system could work for the users of the metaverse. Each user's computer is helping to validate the metaverse's blockchain. The blockchain holds a database of human users. So, only the users that work to validate the blockchain are listed as authentic users.

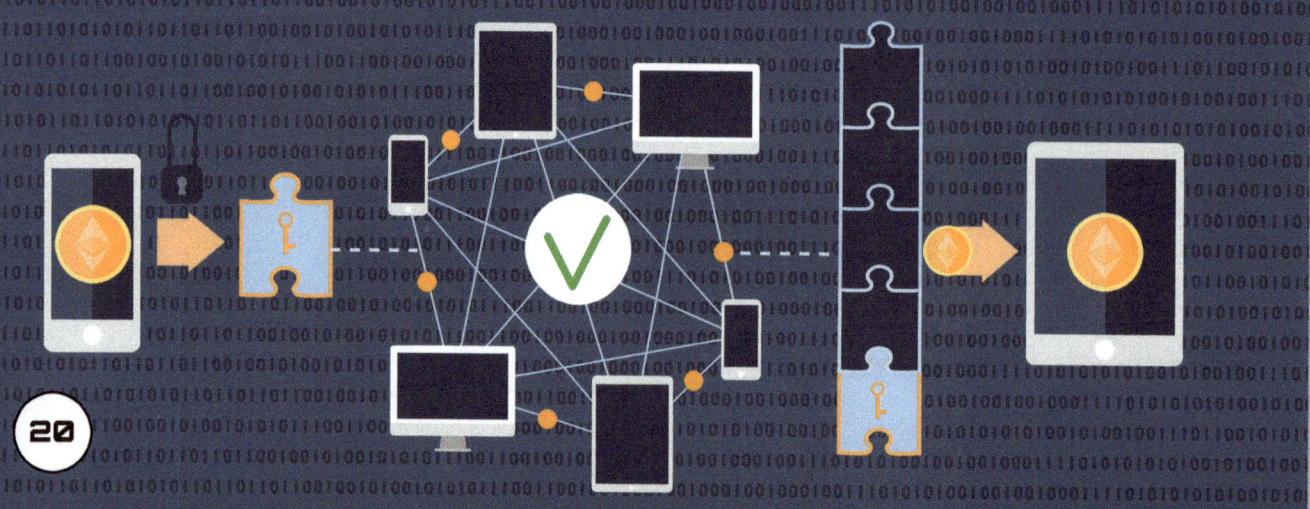

Smart contract. Blockchains are also used to set up fair agreements between people called smart contracts. The agreement can be about anything. Let's say Person 1 agrees to build an **app** for Person 2. Person 2 says they will pay 1 coin when the app is available for download. The agreement is recorded on the blockchain and runs automatically. As soon as the app is downloaded, the contract is validated, and the payment is made. Person 1 cannot be cheated out of their fee, and Person 2 only pays if Person 1 does the job right. Smart contracts work in the real world, but they will be most useful in the metaverse where the work is all happening inside a computer-generated reality!

NFT's. The metaverse has jobs and money, and that money could be a cryptocurrency. The things you buy in the metaverse are also recorded on a blockchain. There is already a system for doing this using NFT's, short for nonfungible tokens. NFT's are unique pieces of code like a crypto coin. The NFT cannot be altered in any way and cannot be copied or replaced. That is what *nonfungible* means—a bitcoin is fungible because they are all alike and one can replace the other. The NFT is maintained and validated on a blockchain, so it can be bought and sold by people. Today, NFT's are linked to online artworks—pictures, videos, or music. The NFT makes a unique, unchangeable link to that art. Of course, art is itself a series of computer codes that can be copied and changed. So in the real world, owning an NFT does not mean you own the art—anyone can see it online! However, things will be different in the metaverse. The NFT means that that art is yours alone.

3 TELEPRESENCE

ALWAYS BEING THERE

The metaverse is a technology that aims to take a person into an alternative reality, leaving their body in the real world. Telepresence makes use of some of the same technologies to do something similar. *Tele* means "from afar." Telepresence technology allows people to be in places far away without having to travel there. What does this mean? Someone talking to you on the phone is not there with you. A person communicating via a video call is not present, either. They can see and hear what is going on in front of the screen but cannot visit another room or have an effect on their surroundings. Telepresence technology allows a person far away to become another person in the room—or anywhere else in the world.

TRAVELING WITHOUT MOVING

Telepresence technology replaces the human body with a robot. The robot allows a person to see and hear what is happening in another location. The person can also control the robot so it moves around that area. It might take some getting used to, but after a while people will treat a telepresence robot just like any other human being.

Being there. Travel is expensive, time-consuming, and damaging to the environment. Telepresence reduces the need for people to travel. However, taking trips can be a lot of fun. People can still travel when they want to see family or friends, for example. The rest of the time, they could make do with being telepresent. In this way, this technology will be of most use for businesspeople. With telepresence, virtual visitors are free to move around and talk to different people in the building or factory, just as if they were there themselves.

Robotic body. A modern telepresence robot is quite simple. It is a video display as a "head." This shows the face of the traveler, and they can see a video feed of wherever the robot is facing. Extra cameras could let them see in all directions at once. The "body" of the robot is a stand that holds the screen and a wheeled platform. The traveler controls the robot from a distant location. As long as a building is accessible, a telepresent visitor can roll around independently for meetings and visits.

Immersive presence. The flat screen view from a simple forward-facing camera can take some getting used to. Fully immersive telepresence using VR technology has also been developed. Instead of seeing and hearing a computer-generated 3D reality, the visitor sees whatever is surrounding the robot far away. Just as VR headsets create 3D vision by showing the eyes two slightly different views, stereoscopic cameras on the robot use two lenses to record two slightly different videos. When viewed in the headset, the image will be seen in three dimensions.

Manipulation. The benefits of a fully immersive telepresence are increased if the robot can pick things up more like a human. Robots capable of this kind of manipulation are not **autonomous,** meaning they cannot move and take hold of objects by themselves. Instead, their movements are controlled by the human user, who just happens to be far away.

TELEROBOTICS

The technology of VR and telepresence can also put a person inside another machine, like a deep-sea submarine or road vehicle. This is an area of technology called telerobotics.

Teleoperation. Telerobotics relies on a human controller operating a robotic vehicle. In the past, this kind of tech was known as remote control. The link between the controller and the robot can be as simple as a wire connection or two-way radio. Modern teleoperation refers to controlling robotic vehicles that are not in view of the operator—and could be on the other side of the world. Here, the communication links are through the internet, cellular network, or via satellite.

UAV's. A well-advanced area of telerobotics is the UAV, which is short for uncrewed aerial vehicles, also known as drones. Drones can be controlled via a flat screen or by using immersive VR. Commercial and leisure drones are generally linked by radio and have a limited range. Most also have a GPS connection, so they can track their route and fly back to the start point automatically if contact with the human controller is lost. Other drones, such as those used by the military, have the range of full-sized aircraft. Here, teleoperation is performed via a satellite link. The pilot flies the UAV from a fully working cockpit that is on the ground. Instead of looking out the window, the pilot's view is through a high-definition video screen.

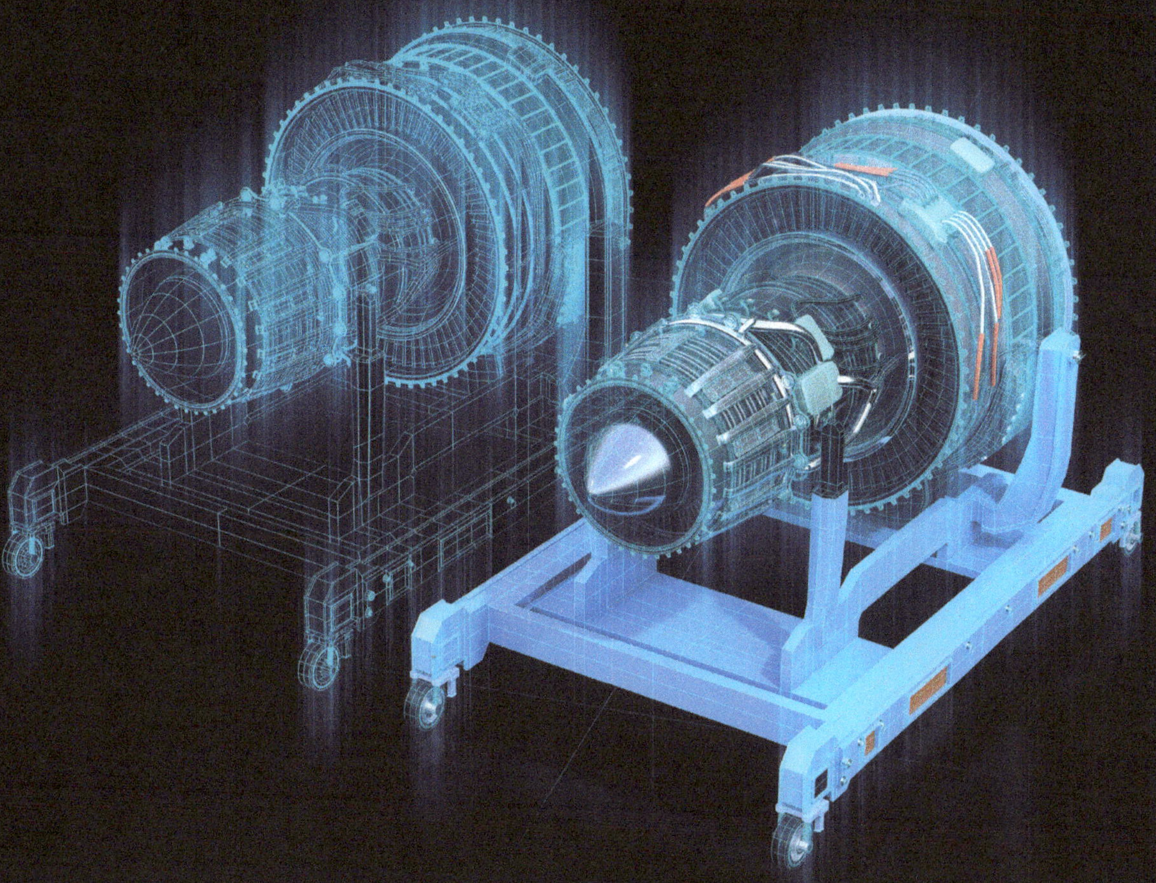

Digital twin. A digital twin is where the technologies of telepresence and the metaverse merge. A digital twin is a virtual copy of a real-world object or system created by a computer. As the name suggests, the digital twin is as near to being identical in its features and behaviors as possible. Digital twins have many uses. For example, they can be used to test processes before they run for real in the physical world or to simulate problems to see how real-world machines might break.

EXPLORERS OF THE FUTURE

Telepresence technology allows explorers to go where no one has gone before. Robots travel to places that are too far for humans to reach or too dangerous for them. A VR system called the CAVE can recreate real places, so people can visit anywhere on Earth—or another planet.

Martian rovers. No humans have visited another planet—yet. The only explorers have been robot rovers, such as NASA's Curiosity and China's Zhurong. The Martian rovers are fitted with stereoscopic video cameras, and controllers back on Earth use these pictures to create three-dimensional views of the red rocks and sand around the rover. They use this VR version of Mars to decide where the rover should go next.

Where people cannot go. Down on Earth, robots are sent into danger in place of humans. They are sent in to investigate unexploded bombs and leaks of radioactivity or into collapsed buildings. Walking robots have also been sent to study volcanoes that are spewing out poisonous gases. Fish robots are exploring the oceans, and snake robots crawl around inside ancient buildings, including the Pyramids of Giza in Egypt.

The CAVE. Short for the Cave Automatic Virtual Environment, this may be a way for anyone to walk on the moon or visit the bottom of the sea. The CAVE is a kind of VR that does not use a headset. Instead, the images of the virtual environment are projected onto the walls, floor, and ceiling of a small room. A motion capture system, similar to the one used by some video game consoles, tracks the movement of the person in the CAVE and alters the view on the walls to match their movements. The user also wears 3D glasses with motion detectors that track the movement of the head. Seen through the 3D glasses, objects appear to float in front of a person in CAVE. The user can walk around the floating object and look at it from all sides.

4 METAVERSE ARCHITECTURE

BUILDING IN THE METAVERSE

Just as architects today design and build the spaces where we live and work, metaverse architecture is the art and technique of designing structures in an immersive digital universe where people can interact virtually with 3D models and objects. Traditional architecture focuses on designing and constructing spaces to work and live. Metaverse architecture focuses on virtual form and geometry using pure creativity—designs are not confined to the real world.

THE METAVERSE LANDSCAPE

The metaverse is designed to take a user away from the body into a new world. However, a person's experiences in the metaverse must be created by others. These include metaverse architects who design the virtual spaces, game designers who create the virtual environments and experiences that users may enjoy, and content creators who produce NFT's and other products that form the basis of a metaverse economy. The metaverse also has virtual **real estate** developers and brokers for land and property brought and sold as NFT's in the virtual landscape.

There is no up or down in the metaverse!

Building in the metaverse. Architecture and real estate in the metaverse will go way beyond the traditional definitions and will require shifting perspectives and learning new skills. Metaverse architecture will involve different layers of technology, such as 3D modeling, AR technology, and geospatial mapping, to create new virtual worlds.

Metaverse real estate is a virtual landscape where people can connect to play games, release products, offer services, and host events. In real-world real estate, the size and location of a plot of land are important factors. These determine how the land may be used. In the metaverse, the size and location of real estate can be designed to meet any need. In the future, people may be hosting more real-world activities on the metaverse, including trade shows, exhibitions, weddings, and other social gatherings. This may reduce the demand for traditional properties used for these purposes.

Metaverse real estate can be purchased similarly to how you would purchase an NFT. Businesses often own these virtual properties. And just like any other type of real estate, they can be bought, sold, purchased, and leased. Today, investors are betting that owning digital plots of land in the metaverse will pay off in the future.

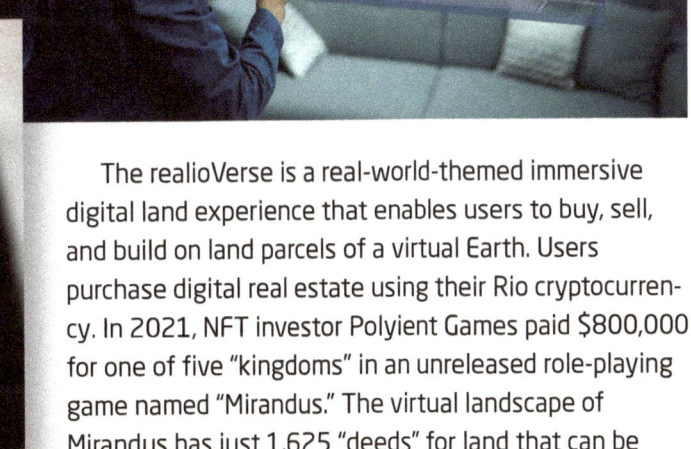

The realioVerse is a real-world-themed immersive digital land experience that enables users to buy, sell, and build on land parcels of a virtual Earth. Users purchase digital real estate using their Rio cryptocurrency. In 2021, NFT investor Polyient Games paid $800,000 for one of five "kingdoms" in an unreleased role-playing game named "Mirandus." The virtual landscape of Mirandus has just 1,625 "deeds" for land that can be purchased and sold just like land in the real world.

5 EVERYDAY LIFE IN THE METAVERSE

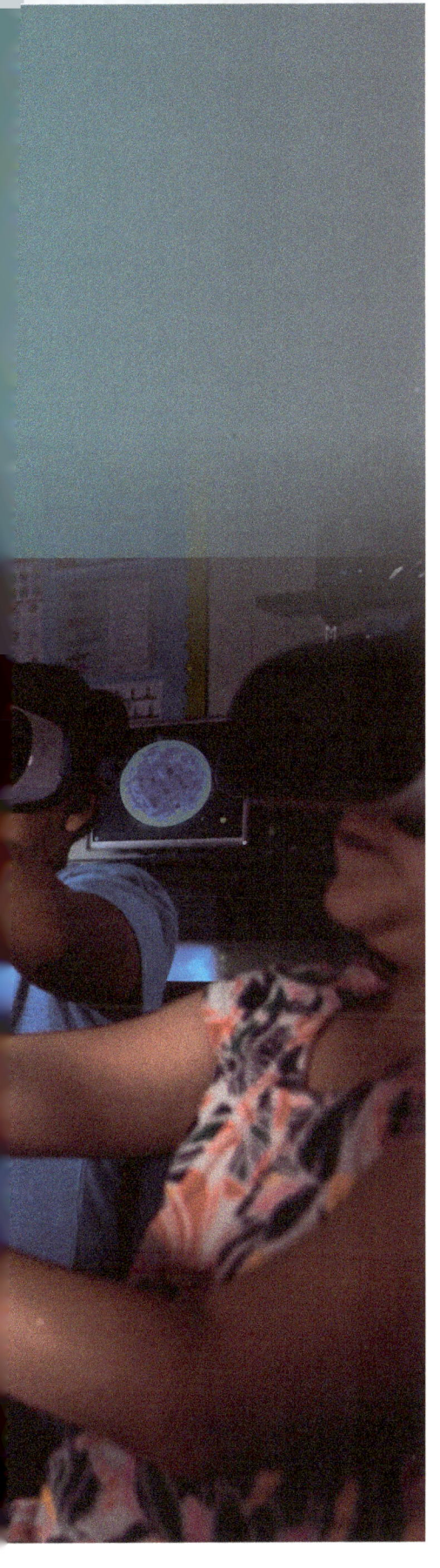

WORK, REST, AND PLAY

What will an ordinary day be like in the metaverse? It cannot all be fun and adventure in a VR world. There will be work to do and lessons to learn. How will that work? The biggest developer of metaverse technology today is the social media company Meta. They have already created some metaverse applications where people can meet with work colleagues or hang out with friends. All that is needed is headsets and a handheld controller—much like the ones used for gaming. The technology is still primitive, especially the way avatars appear and interact in the metaverse. It is hard to see the benefits of it over using more established technologies like video calling or chat apps. However, a VR setup allows anyone to transform their workspace. People without an office space can create their ideal work environment in the metaverse. The same idea could be used in the classroom. Instead of sitting at a desk for lessons, the teacher could take students on trips into the metaverse. Where would you like to go?

AT WORK

The metaverse is not a VR gaming system. To be a success, the metaverse will also need to function as a place where people go to work, make things, and earn money. The metaverse could also be a great place to learn.

Horizon Worlds. The main metaverse app available today is Horizon Worlds. This is developed by Meta, which also owns Facebook and Instagram. Horizon Worlds has been described as a cross between Minecraft and Roblox—games where users can create their own VR environments. But Horizon Worlds is not supposed to be a game. It is supposed to be a way that people and organizations create their own corner of the metaverse, where they can live, work, and meet with other Horizon World users.

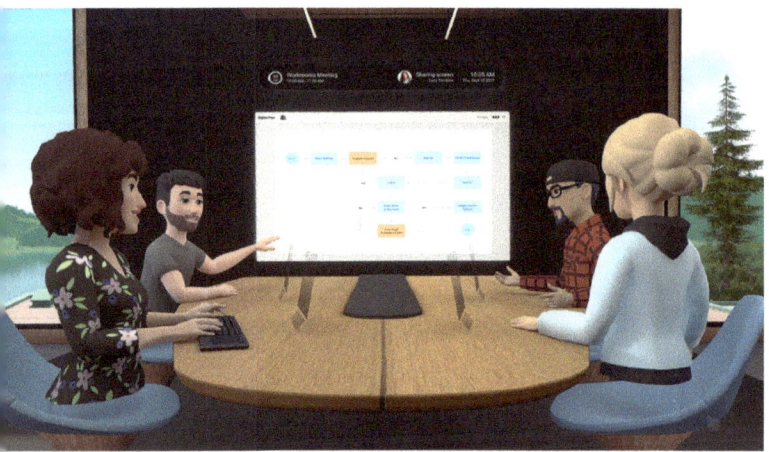

Body problems. The first avatars in Horizon Worlds had no legs. They hovered in the air with a head and arms. That seemed weird. Horizon Worlds now plans to introduce avatars with legs. It is difficult to do this because the basic VR headset and controller have trouble calculating where the legs and arms of the avatar should be located as the user moves around. Horizon Worlds decided that a simplified avatar with no legs was a better option than having avatars that waved their arms and legs in strange ways!

Virtual office. A real-world workspace for many people is simply a desk with space for a keyboard and other devices and a screen. Many people today choose to do their work away from an office building. However, they may not have room for a desk or screen. Instead, they can now set up in the metaverse. In the VR of the metaverse, your desk is big enough to do whatever you want.

At school. Computer technology has already transformed education, but VR and the metaverse might be one of the biggest changes yet. This new technology will have two big impacts. The VR tech will allow students to attend classes anywhere in the world. Millions of children could be given a lesson by an expert scientist, historian, or artist, all at the same time. However, there is more to learning than that. Teachers could take their students into the metaverse to watch historic events play out in real time. It will be as if they were there in person. They could travel into cells or atoms to better understand science, or they could do math assignments that are VR games and puzzles. A day at school could be very cool in the future.

HAVING FUN

When work or school is done, there is still plenty to do in the metaverse. Metaverse leisure activities could be based on entertainment technology already in use. The technology adds to any experience—whether exercising, playing sports, or watching a movie.

Exercise. Running machines and exercise bikes are good to keep active and fit while staying indoors. Many of these machines, such as those made by Peloton, have an interactive feature, where a screen shows live video of a trainer leading the fitness program. Users can also choose a video that shows a running or cycling route anywhere in the world. The video playback matches the speed of the user for a realistic experience. The next step is to add a VR headset to this exercise system. For example, the HOLOFIT app links to a stationary bike or treadmill. The user can choose to take a run around Paris, through snow-capped mountains, or visit an imaginary world. They can even race against other app users.

Smart clothing. Technology embedded in clothing and equipment can help people get better at sports. This so-called smart clothing uses the same kind of motion sensors found in haptic suits to track the position of the body. When the body is out of position, the wearer receives some feedback that helps them fix the problem. For example, the Carv coaching system tracks the position of a skier's feet as they slide downhill. It gives voice instructions to the skier through headphones to help them make turns and travel faster. This kind of smart clothing could make it possible to play sports in the metaverse.

4D. Watching films in the metaverse will be different from the normal 2-dimensional (2D) or even 3D movies you may be used to. A 4-dimensional (4D) movie theater chair adds other senses to the movie-watching experience. The chair rocks and vibrates to match the action. Chemicals are released to create the smells of a scene. Viewers even experience the weather with sprinkles of rain and gusts of wind!

6 SUPER SENSES

SEEING MORE

Humans perceive the world through our five main senses: vision, hearing, smell, taste, and touch. Metaverse and virtual reality technology create worlds that are perceived in the same way, so we see and feel objects and hear sounds as we do in the real world. But why does it have to be that way? VR technology could create worlds where we can see and hear features of the real world that are invisible to our normal senses. We could see heat or pollution and have super-sensitive hearing, or vision that's as powerful as a telescope.

Mixed reality is a blend of VR with the real world. Instead of looking at a screen, we look through it at the real world, but extra features are displayed before our eyes. These features are augmented reality, or AR. *Augmented* means "to make better," and AR technology is a way of merging the online world with this one. One day, we might not even notice the difference between the two.

ADDING SUPERPOWERS

Smell and taste use receptors in the mouth and nose to pick up chemicals that our brain perceives as scent and flavor. Today, it is not possible to recreate these sensations in a virtual reality. However, VR tech could change things up, so we see, or even hear, chemicals that we cannot smell. This may be especially useful when we encounter chemicals that may be poisonous. Other VR applications may allow us to see heat as well as light. VR technology may also be combined with teleoperated robotic suits that give us superstrength. This cool technology could make us superhuman both inside the metaverse and outside of it as well.

Extrasensory detectors. Wearable tech like smartwatches and fitness trackers collect information about the body, such as heart rate and activity levels. Similar devices that look for changes in the environment, such as pollution, toxins, or extreme heat and cold, can also be worn. VR tech could show us where this danger is coming from and sound a warning when we get too close. This kind of technology is best used by emergency workers. Soldiers already rely on night vision technology, which visualizes the heat from objects instead of light. As headset technology improves for the metaverse, we may all have the ability to see in the dark. We could also understand any language using VR technology. Any voices picked up by the headset could be translated by a large language-model AI, into a chosen language—or the words could appear on the screen. In the metaverse, VR technology may give everyone these superpowers.

Exoskeletons. An exoskeleton is a robotic suit worn around the body. They are designed to move with the body, adding extra strength and stamina to the arms and legs. The technology can be life-changing for people with mobility problems. The suit takes over the job of walking and lifting. The suits are also used in warehouses for heavy lifting, and they are being developed by the military so infantry soldiers can move faster and carry more equipment. However, exoskeleton engineers are thinking bigger, such as Prosthesis, which is a superstrength technology designed for racing.

Sensory problems. Even with all the exciting possibilities, spending long periods in the virtual reality of the metaverse will be difficult. Scientists know that our senses are optimal for real-world experiences. In the metaverse, our senses may struggle to adapt. This can cause discomfort and confusion, disrupting the natural rhythm of our lives. For example, the light coming from VR screens does not have the same mix of colors as natural sunlight. Natural light is more yellow compared to artificial light, especially at the beginning and end of the day. The blue light from a computer screen can trick the body into thinking it is still the middle of the day when it is the middle of the night. That confusion can make it harder for people to fall asleep at bedtime.

Our attention in the metaverse, where things look and sound very different compared to the real world, will not be the same. In the metaverse, we are less able to take in all that is going on around us. It can be a confusing place. Sounds in VR need to be louder to get attention in the metaverse. But using headphones turned up loud for too long will damage our hearing.

AUGMENTED REALITY

Augmented reality adds a layer of information over the real world. Instead of a VR headset or goggles, augmented reality works through AR glasses. The user looks through the glasses in the real world, and AR information is projected onto the glass. A smartphone or tablet can also be used for a similar experience. The camera images the real-world screen, and the AR layer is displayed on top of it on the screen.

Giving assistance. AR can add useful information to a real-world scene. Users can call up specific information using voice searches. The AR glasses know their location and can provide general information, such as the weather forecast. AR can add icons to highlight interesting or useful places, such as stores or transit hubs. Eye-tracking systems can detect which icon the eye is focusing on and display a route to that location on the glass.

Using such AR information is not particularly different from using a smartphone today. The greatest benefit is that AR glasses are hands-free, and you do not need to look down at a screen.

AR contact lenses are being developed, but they are currently too expensive to be practical. Battery technology also needs to improve before wearable AR becomes commonplace. Long-lasting AR batteries today are too heavy to wear on your head all day.

Instruction manual. AR is a very useful tool for displaying complex information while working with your hands. Instead of having to own tools and consult instruction manuals printed on paper or a computer screen, a technician can see everything through their AR glasses. This AR layer could show plans for how to construct a machine. A similar system could be used by people making simple repairs to pipes or appliances in the home without having to call a plumber or electrician.

ENGAGE YOUR READER

Nonfiction writing often includes subject-specific vocabulary terms. Knowing the words related to the topic helps us understand the text itself.

When good readers come upon words they don't know well, they pause and try to figure them out. One tool they use is the glossary, like the one on page 4. Not every word can be defined in a glossary, though!

Authors know this, so they leave clues about words in the text. Next time you encounter a challenging word, stop and look for information about its meaning in the surrounding sentences. Sometimes authors define the term right there in the text! Other times, they'll compare the term to something you may already know. Authors even use punctuation like commas or dashes to clue you in to a word's meaning.

INSTRUCTIONS

1. Consider the list of challenge words and identify where each is used in the text. You can use the Index on page 48 to help you locate each term.

2. Explain how the author described each word. Ask yourself "what is happening in the text?" or "how is this word being used?" as you search for clues about their meanings.

3. Create your own definitions of the words. Don't just copy the dictionary definitions. Instead think about how you would tell a friend what each term means.

4. Add a visual representation for each word. Think about what you could draw that will help you remember what the words mean.

Visit www.worldbook.com/resources to download your own graphic organizer as well as other free resources!

CHALLENGE WORDS

- Robotic
- Digital
- Currency
- Immersive
- Architecture
- Avatar
- Code
- Telepresence

EXAMPLE

Challenge Word	Page(s)	Author's Description	Personal Definition	Visual Representation
Robotic	26, 42-43	- automatic - mechanical machine - remote controlled - substitute for human actions	Robotic is when a machine can be controlled to do a task.	
Digital				

INDEX

A
accelerometers, 11
architecture, 30, 31, 32
artificial intelligence, 12
artificial light, 43
augmented reality, 32, 41, 44, 45
authentication, 20

B
banking records, 16
Bitcoin, 16, 17, 19

C
Carv (skiing system), 39
Cave Automatic Virtual Environment, 28, 29
classroom, 35
cockpit, 26
codes, 19, 21
computer, 5, 8, 9, 10, 11, 12, 15, 16, 17, 18, 19, 20, 21, 25, 27, 43, 45
controller, 26, 27, 35, 36
crime, 12, 13
Curiosity (rover), 28
cyberspace, 8

D
database, 18, 19, 20
digital twin, 27
drones, 26

E
electrical power, 17
Ethereum, 16, 17, 19
exercise, 38
exhibitions, 33
exoskeleton, 43
eye-tracking systems, 44

F
feedback, 11, 39
4D movie theater, 39

G
GPS, 26

H
headset, 10, 11, 25, 29, 35, 36, 38, 42, 44
HOLOFIT, 38
Horizon Worlds, 36

I
immersive VR, 26

M
manipulation, 25
Martian rovers, 28
Meta, 35, 36
metaverse, 5, 6, 7, 8, 9, 10, 11, 12, 13, 15, 16, 20, 21, 23, 27, 30, 31, 32, 33, 34, 35, 36, 37, 38, 39, 42, 43
miners (cryptocurrency), 16, 17, 18, 19, 20
money, 9, 15, 16, 18, 21, 36
morals, 13
motion capture, 29
motion sensors, 11, 39

N
Neom (future city), 8
night vision, 42
nonfungible tokens, 21, 33
nonplayer character, 12

P
Peloton, 38
pollution, 17, 41, 42
processor, 5
proof of stake, 19
proof of work, 19
punishment, 13

R
remote control, 26

repairs, 45
robot, 11, 24, 25, 26, 27, 28

S
school, 7, 37, 38
science fiction, 5, 8
screen, 10, 23, 24, 25, 26, 37, 38, 41, 42, 43, 44, 45
senses, 39, 40, 41, 43
smart clothing, 39
smart contract, 21
smells, 39
Snow Crash, 8, 9
Stephenson, Neal, 8
superhuman, 42, 43

T
teleoperation, 26
telepresence, 22, 23, 24, 25, 26, 27, 28
telerobotics, 26
telescope, 41
3D vision, 25
360-degree video, 25
touch, 10, 11, 41
traveler, 24

U
Uncanny Valley, 11
uncrewed aerial vehicles (UAV's), 26

V
validators, 19, 20
video games, 9, 29
virtual Earth, 33
virtual visitors, 24

W
weddings, 33
workspace, 35, 37

Z
Zhurong (rover), 28

www.ingramcontent.com/pod-product-compliance
Lightning Source LLC
Chambersburg PA
CBHW041138170426
43198CB00023B/2984